GW00750469

Catholic Traditionalism

by
Dr Raymond Edwards

All booklets are published thanks to the
generous support of the members of the
Catholic Truth Society

CATHOLIC TRUTH SOCIETY
PUBLISHERS TO THE HOLY SEE

Contents

Catholic Traditionalism

Recently, there has been increased interest amongst Catholics in the older form of Mass, that celebrated prior to the liturgical reforms arising from the Second Vatican Council. It is known by a variety of names: the "Tridentine Rite", old Rite, "Latin Mass", Traditional Latin Mass (TLM), classical Rite, Pian Rite, Gregorian Rite, *usus antiquior*, 1962 Missal (the last revision before the Council), the Extraordinary Form. Pope Benedict recently issued a document enabling priests to celebrate Mass in this form without, as before, needing special permission from their bishops. The aim of this pamphlet is to give the recent history of this form of the Mass, to help those Catholic clergy and laity who are interested in learning more about it, and to describe those bodies and organisations whose primary mission is to promote and celebrate this particular liturgical tradition.

Along the way, however, we will also encounter other groups whose focus, although it includes this liturgical tradition, is broader, and whose relationship with the Church less happy. Some Catholics attached to the old Mass have turned to schismatic groups; I would urge them to consider two things: first, Mass in the older form of the Rite is, or should be, ever more widely available from priests in communion with Rome, which schismatics are not; second, the overall character of the best-known schismatic group, the Society of St Pius X, is (as we shall see below) disquieting.

I have called this essay "Catholic Traditionalism"; as a shorthand term of reference, the description "Traditional Catholics" is often applied, but could be confusing. In a strong sense, all Catholics of whatever liturgical views are "traditional", in that the faith is transmitted by being "handed down" (*traditio* is from the Latin *tradere*, "to hand down"[1]). We are here considering not this issue, which is one of fundamental importance; but the more incidental one of groupings within the Church that exhibit certain liturgical characteristics and preferences. The reader should note that "traditionalism" is here used in this sense only; no reference or allusion is intended to the non-Christian syncretistic philosophy of that name promoted by the French savant René Guénon and his followers.

I should say, in disclaimer, that I have no formal connexion with any of the bodies described here although, some years ago, I used regularly to attend Mass in the older form of the Roman Rite, and have done so sporadically in more recent years.

---

[1] St Paul gives the earliest formulation of this doctrine in 1 Co 15 1-8, esp v.3: I taught you what I had been taught myself; in the Latin Vulgate, *Tradidi enim vobis in primis quod et accepi.*

A Brief History of Liturgical Reform[2]

A casual observer, seeing the liturgical disputes and confusions that have disturbed the Catholic Church in recent decades, might honestly wonder what all the fuss was about. Surely, details of how Mass is celebrated, and in what language, are of secondary importance for the Christian?

There are several reasons why this view is profoundly mistaken. The Liturgy is, above all, something objective: Pope John Paul II said "the Liturgy is never anyone's private property"[3]; it is, also, a central source of Tradition in the Church's sense, forming part of the deposit of faith: as the old tag has it, *lex orandi, lex credendi* - "the Church believes as she prays". The form that the Liturgy takes, then, is neither arbitrary nor without its profound effect on what and how we believe.

The Background to Liturgical Reform

We are often told that, before the Council, "the Mass was the same everywhere". This is not strictly true; within the Catholic Church, there are a variety of Rites long in use to celebrate the Liturgy of the Eucharist: these

---

[2] For a fuller treatment of this topic, see Fr Charles Dilke, *The History of the Mass Explained* (CTS, 2008).

[3] *Ecclesia de Eucharistia*, c.52.

include the Greek and Coptic liturgies of the Eastern Rite churches, and some even more unfamiliar (such as the Chaldean Rite of Addai and Mari). These are all ancient liturgies recognised by the Holy See as valid forms of the Eucharistic celebration. Within the Latin Rite Church - which includes most Catholics in Western Europe, Africa, Asia and the Americas - there is, too, a history of legitimate variety of forms (sometimes called Uses). When the Council of Trent mandated the Pope to reform the Mass in the sixteenth century, a great and often undisciplined variety of liturgical books was in use. After Trent, Pope Pius V took great care in revising the Mass texts; many superfluities and repetitions had crept into the liturgical books, and often even within one diocese a bewildering variety of forms were in use. Most of these were the result of simple confusions in transmission of the texts, inevitable after many centuries of books being copied by hand and circulated locally. The recent invention of printing allowed for a greater uniformity of worship; and so when the reformed texts, the Roman Rite of Mass (often called the Tridentine Rite, after the Latin for Trent), were first published in 1570[4], they were made obligatory on the Latin Rite Church. An exception was made, however, for any form of the Rite that had been in continuous use

---

[4] A second edition in 1604 added the rubrics, giving detailed instructions about the gestures, postures and other actions that accompanied the actual words of the Mass.

for the previous two hundred years. Thus, the Dominican Order retained their individual use, as did the Carthusians; also preserved were the ancient Mozarabic Rite used in parts of Spain, the Ambrosian Rite in Milan, and the Braga Rite in Portugal. England had its own form of the Liturgy, usually known as the Sarum Use (which actually covers several different forms); however since England was by this time no longer officially Catholic, the Sarum Use was no longer widely said. Priests sent to England for the mission were generally trained in the Roman Rite as used in Italy and France.

Local variations aside, the core of the Mass had a long history. The Roman Canon is first found around 350 AD, in substantially the form it still retains. The revised texts printed in 1570 were used largely unchanged for the next four centuries; although, given the state of liturgical scholarship in the sixteenth century, and the way in which the Tridentine books were compiled (from materials hitherto transmitted in manuscript) the text did preserve some features that are demonstrably late accretions.

Growing study of the Liturgy from the seventeenth century on, which took added impetus from the nineteenth century's historical scholarship, gave rise to what is generally called the Liturgical Movement. Its primary goal was to replace what Alcuin Reid has called "pietistic subjectivity" with a truly liturgical piety; one, that is, conformed to the Church's liturgical seasons. Another central aim was to foster what Pius X called *participatio actuosa*. The precise sense given to this phrase is a matter of some debate. To quote Reid again:

"The distinction...is between active (or better, "actual") participation in the Liturgy, and "activist" participation. At the beginning of the twentieth century, activist participation - having as many people as possible doing as much as possible in the liturgical rites so that they are "involved" or "included", such as one so often sees at Masses for children or school groups - was unknown and unimaginable. At the end of the twentieth century, however, it was actual participation - whereby the engagement of the mind and the heart has priority over doing things - that was more likely to be unknown".[5]

More recently, Laurence Hemming has commented:

We have been strongly schooled by the implementation of liturgical reform to interpret *actuosa participatio* as intense, conscious, agent, participation in the rites - the right and ability to say and perform the actions of the liturgy for ourselves. In reality this is about the one thing that *actuosa participatio* cannot mean. It means, rather, fully to participate in what the rite itself participates *in* and makes us present *to*... *Actuosa participatio* is not a

---

[5] From an essay, "The Catholic Liturgy: What happened? What needs to be done?" in *The Catholic World Report*, December 2003.

description of what we must be *doing*, but a synonym for our life in the Spirit...[6]

The beginning of the Liturgical Movement is usually placed at a 1909 conference in Malines, in Belgium (although the nineteenth century French Benedictine Dom Prosper Guéranger's studies were an essential precursor). The movement's focus was within French- and German-speaking monastic communities[7]; there was less presence in mainstream parish life. Moreover, it had little impact in the English-speaking world, particularly in England[8]. This is undoubtedly due in part to the majority Protestantism of these countries and, in the case of Great Britain, to a rooted liturgical conservatism that valued supremely the form of the Mass for which the martyrs of the penal times had died.

In continental Europe, however, various elements of the Liturgical Movement's programme were, during the course of the twentieth century, incorporated into celebrations of the Liturgy, either officially or on an ad hoc basis. Some of these (such as the widespread use of people's missals) were an unequivocally good thing; others arguably less so.

---

[6] *Worship as a Revelation: The Past, Present, and Future of Catholic Liturgy* (Continuum, 2008) pp.31-32.

[7] Important names here include the Belgian Dom Lambert Beauduin, the German Odo Casel at Maria Laach, and the German secular priest Romano Guardini.

[8] It is difficult to think of English Catholics who can be described as active in the liturgical movement, except perhaps for Fr Adrian Fortescue, who (in this as in much else) was an eccentric figure.

There was a trend in some countries for "dialogue Masses", where the responses generally made by the server to the priest were now made by the congregation as a whole. There is much to be said in favour of this, but it can suggest that the essence of "participation" is found in activity or speech, rather than in prayerful awareness of what is being celebrated. Less happy was the practice, these days almost universal, of the priest celebrating Mass *versus populum* - facing the people rather than, as hitherto, facing the same way as the congregation, liturgical East, towards the rising sun as a type of the Risen Christ. This change was presented as a return to the practice of the early Church, although the evidence adduced in favour of this being a primitive practice now seems distinctly flawed[9].

In 1951, Pope Pius XII introduced a series of changes, which were first optional, and from 1956 compulsory for the whole Latin Rite Church, in the celebration of the Easter Liturgy, the summit of the Church's year. The most important change was restoring the Easter Vigil to being celebrated at night; previously, it was generally celebrated on the morning of Holy Saturday. This, again, is generally considered a good thing; not so was the simultaneous decision to reduce the number of readings in the Vigil from twelve to four (the reformed Rite of 1970 has restored most of these, and has nine in all).

---

[9] For a detailed consideration of this point, see U M Lang, *Turning Towards the Lord* (Ignatius Press, 2004)

Liturgical reform was high on the agenda of the Second Vatican Council when it met in 1962. On 4th December 1963, the Council promulgated its first official document, the Constitution on the Sacred Liturgy, known (like all the Magisterium's documents) by the first two words of its Latin text, *Sacrosanctum Concilium*. The Constitution draws extensively on the work of the Liturgical Movement, and then current liturgical scholarship. It is concerned more with general principles than with the minutiae of any reform, which it entrusted to "experts" and the consultation of bishops. The aim of the reforms is set out in a paragraph it is worth quoting in full:

> The Ordinary of the Mass (*Ordo Missae*) is to be revised in a way that will reveal more clearly the real function of each of the parts and the connexions of the various parts with one another. This revision is also to facilitate the devout, active participation of the faithful.
>
> To this end, while the substance of the rites is to be preserved, they themselves should be simplified. Doublets and any additions of little value that have accrued in the course of the centuries are to be omitted. Certain things that have fallen out through the wearing processes of time are to be reinstated after the ancient model of the holy Fathers, according as they may seem advisable or necessary[10].

---

[10] Par. 50. The next 7 paragraphs give guidelines about some specific changes.

The document also includes a definite caveat, however:

Innovations should not be made unless when a real and definite advantage will accrue to the Church and when due care has been taken to ensure that the new forms shall, as it were, grow out organically from those already existing. (par.23)

This reform, the Council directed should happen "as soon as possible" (par.25)

The Mass is Reformed

Pope Paul VI at once set up a committee, known as the Consilium, to implement these proposed reforms. It was headed by Msgr Annibale Bugnini, a man who has become a lightning rod for traditionalist objections to the reform of the Mass[11]. The Consilium was undoubtedly given rather a free hand by Paul VI, who intervened personally on several occasions to overcome the objections of several of the more conservative Curial cardinals. But to represent it, as is sometimes done, as a cabal of crypto-Protestants setting about them with the liturgical equivalent of a wrecking ball, is a picture that can

---

[11] He is widely stated, on frankly insufficient evidence, to have been a closet Freemason. His prolix memoirs (*The Reform of the Liturgy 1948-1975*, Liturgical Press, 1990) do show him to have been perhaps overly concerned with his own significance, and in all likelihood he made a nuisance of himself to some influential people. This, rather than any supposed revelation of his membership of a Lodge, is the most probable explanation of his sudden demotion in 1975 from his position as Secretary to the Congregation for Rites and appointment as Pro-Nuncio to Iran.

be dispelled by a glance at the list of its members. These included the eminent French Oratorian Louis Bouyer and the Austrian Jesuit Josef Jungmann; no one familiar with their writings could suppose these charges justified[12].

In October 1967, the Consilium presented its work. Mass was celebrated according to the revised Rite before the Synod of Bishops then gathered in Rome. This "trial version" (sometimes called the *missa normativa*) caused some surprise. The nature and degree of the changes made to the Mass were more extensive than generally predicted, and raised in some minds questions about the theology implicit in the reformed Rite[13]. Arguably, the reforms made went considerably beyond what *Sacrosanctum Concilium* intended or the Council Fathers had envisaged. Cardinal Heenan, Archbishop of Westminster, who was privately sceptical of the tendency of the reforms, spoke in the subsequent Synod debate:

---

[12] There has been very extensive discussion, however, on the particular character of the reforms in the light of advances in historical scholarship of the liturgy since their day. Arguably, some of what they supposed were primitive features of the Mass obscured by later developments and thus to be restored in the reform, have been subsequently shown to be late or untypical (this applies especially to features taken from the so-called *Apostolic Traditions* formerly ascribed to Hippolytus). A good introduction to this topic is Fr Thomas Kosik's *Reform of the Reform?* (Ignatius Press, 2003); see also Aidan Nichols, *Looking at the Liturgy* (Ignatius Press, 1996).

[13] The assembled bishops voted on the reform; of the 187 votes, 78 (42%) were wholly in favour, 62 (34%) in favour but with reservations, and 43 (24%) opposed. Four bishops abstained. Three quarters of the Synod, then, approved the reform.

"After studying the so-called Normative Mass it was clear to me that few of [the Consilium] can have been parish priests. I cannot think anyone with pastoral experience would have regarded the sung Mass as being of first importance. At home it is not only women and children but also fathers of families and young men who come regularly to Mass. If we were to offer them the kind of ceremony we saw yesterday in the Sistine Chapel we would soon be left with a congregation of mostly women and children[14].

The official text of the reformed Roman Rite of Mass (*Novus Ordo Missae*) was promulgated on 3rd April 1969 by the Apostolic Constitution *Missale Romanum*. The finally approved texts were substantially identical to the *missa normativa* trialled two years earlier.

The Nature of the Reforms

What, in fact, are the main differences between the older Rite of Mass and the reformed version? The reformed Rite of Mass does indeed look externally rather different from the older form. The first difference that generally strikes anyone

---

[14] Quoted in Scott M P Reid, *A Bitter Trial* (St Austin Press, 2000), which contains an interesting collection of letters between Heenan and Evelyn Waugh, and some of Heenan's public statements on the Liturgy. It brings out well Heenan's ambivalent attitude towards liturgical reform: privately sceptical, but publicly supportive. Conspiracy theorists would probably detect here the malign hand of his sometime secretary, Msgr Derek Worlock.

who (like the majority of today's Catholics) knows only the reformed Rite is that the older form is celebrated wholly in Latin (even, in most cases, the lectionary readings); but we should remember that the original reformed Rite was wholly in Latin too (the growing use of the vernacular is discussed below). The same is true about the direction in which Mass is celebrated (facing east or facing the people) - the current practice of celebrating Mass with the priest facing the people, rather than facing east (pejoratively, and unfairly, described as "turning his back to the congregation", whereas he is actually, like them, turning "towards the Lord") was not part of the original reforms.

As well as these externals, there are some textual differences between the two. The older form opens with an extended series of "prayers at the foot of the altar" (based around an antiphonally recited Psalm) before the Introit or Entrance Antiphon; it also typically ended with the "Last Gospel" (usually most of the first chapter of John) and additional prayers after the final blessing; all of this is omitted by the reformed Rite. The Offertory prayers in the reformed Rite are also different, being both shorter and partly modelled on Jewish "table blessings"; whereas those in the older form of Rite are longer, and stress more the notion of the Eucharistic sacrifice (which is however explicitly mentioned in the reformed prayers). The Eucharistic Prayer in the older Mass (where it is usually called the Canon of the Mass) had only one form (which is now Eucharistic Prayer I) which was always spoken *sotto voce*; the reformed Rite added three others (newly composed, but based in part on patristic models) in addition to the Roman Canon, and directed that they were to be said aloud[15]. Another palpable difference is that the responses to the priest were, in the reformed Rite, to be made by the whole congregation rather than, as in the older form, by the acolyte or acolytes (altar server(s)) on their behalf; the congregation was also mandated to join the priest in the main sung parts of the Mass, the Kyrie (Lord, have mercy) Gloria, and Agnus Dei (Lamb of God), even where these were said rather than sung. Previously, these parts of the Mass were said by the priest and server alone, as was the Confiteor (I confess). Lastly, the reformed Rite also includes a Sign of Peace to be exchanged amongst the congregation (something that many people found and find a particular source of difficulty, for reasons that are cultural rather than theological)[16]. The Sign of Peace in the older

---

[15] There have been a number of additional Eucharistic Prayers for particular needs and occasions issued subsequently (for Reconciliation, for Masses with children and others); these were generally first authorized by local Bishops' Conferences and later by Rome.

[16] These are the main differences between the Ordinary (invariable) parts of the different forms of Mass (there are also some other minor differences, mainly in some of the priest's prayers from the older Rite that the newer one omits); the reformed Rite also came with a greatly expanded Lectionary (three years' worth of readings for Sundays, and two for weekdays, rather than the previous single annual cycle) and a thorough revision of the Proper prayers (collects and the like) including some newly composed alongside the older prayers.

form of the Rite was usually seen only at Solemn High Mass and exclusively between the clergy; its presence in the reformed Rite is because the reformers took as their model of the Mass the solemn, sung High Mass of the older form, not the purely spoken "Low Mass" which would, for most laity in most parishes, have been far more familiar.

All in all, the textual differences between the two forms although numerous are not in fact of huge theological significance (although as we shall see some have argued otherwise); but the experience of attending Mass can be quite different. Even where Mass is still in Latin, and not celebrated facing the people, the congregation in the reformed Rite takes a verbally much more active role; responses that could previously have been made only mentally are now said aloud, and in common[17]. Many find this a help to their participation in the liturgy; others experience it as a distraction. Again, the older form of Mass has substantially larger periods of complete or relative silence; some find this helps their liturgical prayer; others, used to the reformed Rites, find this alienating or simply tedious. But all of these things are, arguably, not of the essence of the Liturgy: although there is a variety in externals between the older and newer forms of the Roman Rite, there is a clear continuity between the fundamental form and meaning of the Liturgy: the Mass remains the Mass.

---

[17] This had been a feature of the "dialogue Masses" mentioned earlier, but these were not especially common before the Council.

Objections to the Reform

The older school of theologians and bishops were concerned by what they saw as the theology implied by the new Order of Mass, and by the General Instruction (usually abbreviated *GIRM*: a technical guide to the rubrics and particulars of celebrating Mass using the revised Rite) prefaced to it. This concern received its most public airing in an open letter addressed to the Pope by a "Group of Roman Theologians[18]", written in June 1969 and published on September 25th, with a covering letter from Cardinal Ottaviani, former Prefect of the Holy Office (now the Congregation for the Doctrine of the Faith). This document, usually known as "The Ottaviani Intervention", has assumed a prominent place in subsequent critiques of liturgical reform.

It begins well enough, making the sensible point that what "the Christian people" wanted was a deeper understanding of the existing liturgy, not a liturgy simplified to make it easier to understand. As its argument develops, however, the justice of its claims is less clear. The reformed Rite of Mass (which it refers to as the *Novus Ordo*, a description commonly used thereafter by many traditionalists) was, it claims, "rejected in substance by the Synod". This, as we have seen, is not true. It then claims

---

[18] One of them was later sacked from his Roman teaching post and taught at Marcel Lefebvre's renegade seminary in Switzerland. It has been claimed that Lefebvre was the organizing hand behind the entire project.

that *GIRM* "reduces the Mass to a 'supper'", an assembly presided over by a priest. Moreover, because *GIRM* does not explicitly mention the Real Presence and Sacrifice, it implicitly denies them. The removal of several prayers from the Rite, and the suppression of various gestures, purifications, and altar cloths is an "implicit repudiation" of the Real Presence; it has compromised the nature of the Mass as a sacrifice and conflated Christ's Real Presence in the Eucharist with his spiritual presence in the Word and the assembly. Omitting the intercalated phrase "*Mysterium Fidei*" from the words of consecration in the Eucharistic Prayers, and using an abbreviated form of "do this in memory of me" encourages (it claims) belief in the Mass as a mere memorial. The reformed Rite as a whole confuses the roles of faithful and priest.

The substantive points made by the Ottaviani document are almost all arguments from absence, built on what it calls the "desacralising omissions" of the reformed Rite. For these to be in any way conclusive, they would (surely) need some positive statement of the doctrines the Ottaviani text presumes underlie them. This positive evidence is simply lacking, and "Ottaviani" is forced back into simple assertion:

> "Participation in the immolation of Christ the Victim will turn into a philanthropists' meeting or a charity banquet".

It also accuses the reformed Rite of "paschalism" and "eschatologism" for allegedly excessive emphasis on Easter, the Resurrection, and the Second Coming; a charge that, to anyone familiar with the Eucharistic teachings of the Church Fathers, is simply bizarre[19].

I have dwelt on this text at some length because it contains, in kernel, the vast majority of the objections to the reformed Rite of Mass typically brought by those traditionalists who refuse to see it as a valid form. We need not suppose their arguments are borrowed directly from the Ottaviani text, but they are substantially identical and are equally patient of the counter-arguments I have outlined[20].

---

[19] One of the authorities cited by the Ottaviani text is Fr Louis Bouyer. Presumably the author(s) had not read, or understood, Bouyer's book *Life and Liturgy* (1954; English translation, 1956), where the centrality of Easter, and the anticipated *parousia*, to all celebrations of the Eucharist is very clearly explained. Whether one accepts Bouyer's arguments, it is curious to cite him in support at one point, and attack him (or positions he had strongly advocated) at another.

[20] They can be found, in essence, for example, in Lefebvre's *Open Letter to Confused Catholics* (English translation, Fowler Wright, 1986). One point the Ottaviani document does make well concerns "busyness" in the reformed Rite: "Then there is the distracting atmosphere created in the church: the ceaseless comings and goings of priest, deacon, subdeacon, cantor, commentator...of lectors (men and women), of servers or laymen welcoming people at the door and escorting them to their places, while others carry and sort offerings." In fairness, I have witnessed equally "busy" celebrations in the older form, with the added distraction of elaborate precedences and choreography. There is (surely) no virtue in itself in a crowded sanctuary.

The Pope forwarded the Ottaviani text to the CDF for their comments; they answered that they were satisfied that the General Instruction was theologically orthodox. Nevertheless, when the new Missal was finally published in March 1970, the Introduction had been changed and amplified in a manner reflecting the criticisms raised. The reformed Rite of Mass itself, as we have seen, was not altered.

We may agree with the CDF, against Ottaviani and those who take him as a champion, that there is nothing doctrinally incorrect about the reformed Rite. Some commentators have argued that elements of the reformed Rite express a theology that, compared to the older form, is deficient - that is, lacking an explicit statement of Church's traditional Eucharistic belief in all its nuance and richness. Others strongly disagree, and argue that the implicit theology of the reformed Rite is equally full. Most informed critics would agree that much of this theology does not find its way into some vernacular versions of the Mass (the current English translation is notorious in this respect). Nevertheless, the reformed Rite of Mass expresses a Eucharistic theology that is thoroughly orthodox. It has, moreover, been solemnly confirmed and authorised by the Church's Magisterium, in the person of several Popes; no Catholic has genuine grounds to deny assent to these reforms. Nevertheless, it is certainly true that many commentators and liturgists at the time and since have spoken as if it was only with these reforms that the Roman Rite escaped the corruption of centuries and became something that could truly nourish the faith of the Christian people. Such talk, to quote Alcuin Reid, "both fails to accord those reforms a fair historical analysis, and makes the ultimate archaeological (and Protestant) claim: that the Catholic Liturgy has been fundamentally defective for over a thousand years". As history and theology, this is simple nonsense.

The Reforms in Practice

During the early 1970's, progressive liturgists introduced a series of innovations, without mandate from the Council's documents. These were generally authorised by the Holy See, often retrospectively. They include:

a) exclusive use of the vernacular. *Sacrosanctum Concilium* does not envisage this; Latin, it says, should be maintained as the primary language of the liturgy, although "some considerable space" should be given to the vernacular, particularly in the readings[21]; Cardinal Arinze has since said, "Vatican II did not abolish Latin[22]". Serious questions remain about the accuracy, and theological completeness, of some vernacular translations (including that into English).

b) communion in the hand. This was introduced without permission in a number of countries; in 1969, Rome reluctantly regularised the position, allowing the practice where it was already established. In England and Wales,

---

[21] par.36 1,2

[22] Introduction to *Sacrosanctum Concilium*, p.6 (CTS, 2004)

although it was practically unknown, in 1976 the hierarchy applied for and received permission for this and it soon became very widespread, largely because of the efforts of progressivist clergy and the acquiescence of an often bewildered laity[23].

c) celebration *versus populum*. This is envisaged as a possibility in the 1970 *GIRM* (and most English translations of it give the impression that it is the norm) but it has been plausibly argued that the text in fact presupposes celebration *ad orientem*, with turning *versus populum* only expected in those parts of the Mass where the priest addresses the congregation directly[24]. The current

---

[23] *Redemptionis Sacramentum* (par.92) and par.161 of the *General Instruction* to the 3rd Edition of the *Missale Romanum* (2000; English translation, 2005) confirm that communion in the hand is allowed only where local Bishops' Conferences have requested and received permission; communion on the tongue remains the universal default norm.

[24] Par.262 of the 1970 *GIRM* states that altars should be freestanding to allow celebration facing the people; several previous paragraphs, however (pars.107, 115-116, 122, 198-199) seem to presuppose celebration *versus orientem*, as the speak of the priest turning to face the people or back to face to the altar. The most widely available English translation of the 1970 *GIRM*, however, omits pars. 77-141 and 159-239 as "detailed directives on the celebration of the Mass"; par.262 however is retained. This enables an arguably mistaken view of the 1970 *GIRM* to be held, that it mandated celebration *versus populum* as the norm; rather than, what would be the more natural reading of the complete text, celebration *versus orientem* as the norm but celebration *versus populum* as a possibility. See Moyra Doorly, *No Place for God* (Ignatius Press, 2007) pp.47-51 for details. The 2000 *GIRM*, however, gives celebration facing the people full status as an equivalently valid option.

ubiquity of celebration *versus populum* is the result of a prevalent fad, or deliberate misunderstanding, rather than the Council's, or even the Consilium's, intention.

Note that none of these features are intrinsic to the reformed Rite; it is perfectly possible, and licit, for Mass according to the 1970 books to be celebrated wholly or substantially in Latin, *ad orientem*, and with communion given only on the tongue[25]. That these options are met only infrequently reflects deficiencies in priests' liturgical formation rather than in the reformed Rite itself. In each case, however, the manner in which these novelties were introduced (generally by instructions from locally constituted Liturgy Commissions without much if anything by way of consultation of the laity) gave as much scandal as the changes themselves.

In a different category altogether are actual abuses and breaches even of the comparatively flexible rubrics of the 1970 *GIRM*; it is not necessary to particularise these horrors, which can be found fully described elsewhere, merely to note that the scandal they gave to many of the faithful only added to the suspicion in the minds of many perfectly sensible Catholics that there was something deeply awry with the liturgical reform. The wanton destruction of ecclesiastical furnishings, some of considerable artistic merit, carried out under the catch-all description of "re-ordering" under

---

[25] This was exactly the practice, for one of the regular Sunday Masses, at the parish I attended as a schoolboy.

the pretext of making churches fit for the reformed liturgy, added to the general impression that something akin to Mao's Cultural Revolution was taking place.

At the same time, there was a major crisis in the Church's sense of identity. Vocations to the priesthood fell precipitously, seminary formation was often in chaos, and priests and religious left the Church in droves. Many saw, and see, liturgical reform as the cause of all this, and of lapsations, of falling numbers of baptisms, and of the parlous state of religious knowledge amongst Catholics today. But liturgical chaos, or ignorance, is (I submit) not a cause but a symptom of a deeper problem: the collapse of catechesis. This may be more justly blamed on the wholesale and unhappy adoption of the educational ideas of the 1960s than on the reformed Liturgy. Catholic schools now struggle to impart a fraction of the catechetical knowledge that, forty years ago, would have been considered utterly basic. Ongoing adult catechesis, reviving which was one of the Council's main goals, is (with some marked exceptions, mostly found amongst the so-called "New Movements") now more likely to take the form of bland and undirected "faith-sharing" with minimal dogmatic content than anything more substantial.

In one sense, certainly, we can link this to liturgical reform: when Mass was largely in Latin, and in an outwardly more complex form, the basic instruction given to catechumens, or those preparing for First Communion, was necessarily fuller and more rigorous, because without it the shape, nature and meaning of the Liturgy would be opaque. Many now seem to assume that, with Mass in the vernacular, these things are so open and obvious as to need little further explanation. The result of this deficient instruction is precisely the lack of awareness of the sacred character of the Mysteries that leads to the frequent irreverences many find so scandalous. The real scandal, I suggest, is that these things generally arise from simple ignorance.

The Preservation of the older Rite

Whatever the truth of this, there was still a widespread desire to retain the option of celebrating Mass in the older form. In England this desire was especially strong, or widespread, or vocal and organised (perhaps, indeed, all of these things at once). In November 1971, then, Cardinal Heenan obtained a Papal Indult for England and Wales, allowing local bishops there to permit celebration of older form of the Roman Rite on specific occasions. This gave much cause for grumbling to progressive liturgists, many (perhaps most) of whom wished to see the older form of the Rite conclusively suppressed[26]. Some bishops were sympathetic to the Indult; others, and their liturgical pundits, have been consistently hostile and

---

[26] Archbishop Bugnini has much to say about the "Heenan Indult" in his autobiography.

obstructive. Nevertheless, there has since that time been a continuing tradition of older Rite celebrations throughout this country.

It was in France, however, that concern for the implications of abandoning the older form of Mass was fiercest. This combined with worries about the quality of seminary formation and catechesis, so, when Archbishop Marcel Lefebvre, former Superior General of the Holy Ghost Fathers, a missionary order, opened a traditionalist seminary (in Switzerland, but largely taking French or French-speaking candidates) he met with considerable interest[27].

In 1974, the Congregation for Divine Worship (in which Msgr Bugnini was still prominent) issued a note reminding bishops that only the newer liturgical books should be used; an exception was made only for priests whose age or ill-health made adapting to the newer books difficult: these were permitted to retain the use of the 1962 Missal, but only for Masses without a congregation. This official disapproval, or at best discouragement, contributed to the defensive "ghetto" mentality found amongst many traditionalists.

In October 1984, the CDW issued another document, *Quattuor Abhinc Annos*, allowing any bishop to extend permission to celebrate Mass according to the older books, much as in England and Wales; securing this permission,

---

[27] I give a fuller account of Lefebvre and his movement in the chapter on p. 46

however, often involved considerable bureaucracy and was thus (as in England) easily impeded by the unsympathetic.

In 1988, Marcel Lefebvre led his followers, the Society of St Pius X (henceforth abbreviated SSPX), into schism by consecrating four bishops without Papal mandate[28]. The Papal motu proprio announcing (and lamenting) this, *Ecclesia Dei Adflicta*, also called for "wide and generous" implementation of the existing provision for the older form of Mass extended under the 1984 document, and established a Pontifical Commission (known, after the document, as the Ecclesia Dei Commission) to monitor and supervise this provision, and to co-ordinate Rome's relations with traditionalist bodies. Implementation of this by diocesan bishops, however, remained very patchy; many were and are content to cede their oversight of liturgy to liturgical committees, typically dominated by those, laity or clergy, markedly hostile to the older Mass.

In all the foregoing, we can distinguish two strands amongst those attached to the older form of the Rite: objections to the manner in which the reforms were implemented, and the widespread abuses that accompanied (and accompany) this; and objections to the very nature of the reforms themselves (the Ottaviani camp). In recent years the relevant dicasteries of the Vatican have been very attentive to the first of these concerns; a series of

---

[28] Again, see p. 46 for a fuller account.

documents have aimed to remedy abuses - *Redemptionis Sacramentum*, *Sacramentum Caritatis*, and, on the subject of vernacular translations, *Liturgiam Authenticam*. We may also notice Pope John Paul II's *Ecclesia de Eucharistia* of 2003, and the new *GIRM* of 2000 (English edition 2005) which, incidentally, is at pains to describe the Mass as a sacrifice. Whilst these documents have been and are still in many places ignored, there is some sign that the era of liturgical free-for-all may be ending. There are, also, definite moves at various levels (from the Papacy down) towards encouraging and recovering the use of Latin in the reformed Rite.

This leaves us, then, with the other strand: those who in varying degrees unhappy with the very nature of the reformed Rite. John Paul II wrote, in 1988

"Some have received the new books with a certain indifference, or without trying to understand the reasons for the changes; others, unfortunately, have turned back in a one-sided and exclusive way to the previous liturgical forms which some of them consider to be the sole guarantee of certainty in the faith"[29].

The most recent Papal document on the Liturgy is aimed in part at exactly this concern. On 7th July 2007, Pope Benedict issued a long-awaited motu proprio, *Summorum Pontificum*, which allowed any priest of the Roman Rite

---

[29] *Vicesimus Quintus Annus*, 14

to celebrate Mass according to the 1962 books without needing special permission to do so, and encouraged priests to be generous in responding to requests from the faithful for Mass in this form. In effect, the document re-iterates that the older form of Mass (which it dubs the Extraordinary Form) is a permanently valid form of the Roman Rite, although the renewed texts of 1970 remain the Ordinary - that is, the usual - form of this Rite. One of the Pope's goals is to promote cross-pollination between the older and the newer forms, encouraging their "mutual enrichment"; this should help the reformed Rite to be seen as truly in the continuous tradition of the Roman Liturgy, and, by allowing it to be enriched and modified under the influence of the older from, make its place in that tradition more secure.

Another aim of the document is to prevent the unnecessary obstruction of the older form of the Rite by those who have been historically opposed to its continuance. It does this by removing the decision as to who may celebrate this form, and when, from bishops and giving it to individual priests. Nevertheless, there have been numerous attempts by various bishops (including several in Great Britain) to obstruct the implementing of this document, by insisting that any priest who wants to offer Mass in the older Form must surmount unnecessary and unrealistic conditions (whether of linguistic proficiency or supposed public demand) that are nowhere specified in the motu proprio itself. These are, in fact, simple instances of local bishops, and their tame liturgists and canon lawyers, acting beyond their competence in a matter that has been explicitly taken out of their hands by the Holy See. The Ecclesia Dei Commission, which has been entrusted with overseeing the motu proprio's implementation, is expected to issue a text in the near future that will clarify these points in a fashion that will not be patient of these misreadings.

A Conclusion, and a Reminder

It is not my business here to adjudicate between competing versions of liturgical history, or offer a considered verdict on the theological points at issue; I have attempted merely to summarise the relevant facts and to suggest an interpretation of them. It is undoubtedly true that amongst those attached to the older form of the Roman Rite are some, not exclusively amongst the clergy, who have what in secular terms could be called a fondness for dressing up; a fad for minutiae of vestments and lace, nostalgia for the high ceremonial of the bygone Papal court. But this is not the whole picture, or even most of it. There is an arguably larger field for excesses of this nature in the older form of Mass; but the majority of celebrations according the 1962 books are sober and undemonstrative. The older rubrics are marginally more complex than the newer ones; but they are, too, in practice more likely to be followed with some care and attention. If all celebrations of the newer form of

Mass were equally attentive, we should not hear so much about the supposed rubrical labyrinth of the older form.

Nor is it true that Mass in the newer form is the carefree liturgical and theological free-for-all supposed by some advocates of the older books. The comparative latitude of the rubrics of the reformed Rite, and the liberty it allows the celebrant to extemporise commentary or explanation, can, it is true, be seen as enabling illicit creativity. Certainly, there are some Masses that are (in defiance of the rubrics and the repeated instructions of the competent offices of the Magisterium) disfigured by improvisation, "dance" or similar infantile gimmicks; and some modern makers of vestments have a fondness for horrible fabrics and simplistic symbolism. But, again, it is eminently possible to attend Mass celebrated according to the newer books in a manner characterised by decorum and punctilio. Lapses into bad taste, or defective theology, are not the exclusive property of either end of the spectrum. Pope Benedict has clearly affirmed that both forms of the Roman Rite are valid, and valuable; an occasion to celebrate legitimate diversity rather than to turn into totems or fetishes for a particular ecclesiological party. Again, it is arguable that "actual participation" means rather different things in the different forms of the Roman Rite, or at least expresses itself in different ways; but to suppose that the congregation at Mass according to the 1962 books does nothing except watch and engage in private devotions, or that those at the newer form must forever be usurping properly clerical functions in order to feel "engaged", is in both cases to caricature rather than describe. Besides, the Mass is not a forum for us to explore or act out our particular vision of ourselves as a worshipping community, but the occasion for us to encounter Christ or, more properly, for Him to meet us. If we forget this, we have forgotten everything.

Catholic Traditionalists Today

This chapter gives brief accounts of those organisations, orders, and foundations that are primarily dedicated to celebrating the older form of the liturgy, and remain in communion with Rome. Although it cannot claim to be exhaustive, it covers the most important and best-known of these bodies. Contact details for the most useful of these can be found under *Further Information*, p.78.

It is important to note that, although the unifying factor here is liturgical, many of those involved in these bodies are also remarkable for their faithful witness to the Church's traditional moral teaching; whilst there may not be an exact causal relationship between liturgy and the moral life, there is a clear and strong correlation.

Organisations in Great Britain

Latin Mass Society of England & Wales

The Latin Mass Society (LMS) was founded in 1965 before the liturgical changes had been implemented or even announced, but when rumours of their likely nature (particularly, the permission to celebrate Mass in the vernacular) were widespread. It is thus the oldest, and probably the best-organised, of any of the traditionalist groups worldwide. It is also unusual in that it is primarily an organisation of the laity, although there are many clerical members, and operates through existing parochial and diocesan structures rather than through a separate network of parishes or clergy of its own. This structural feature, however, does mean that its success in a diocese has hitherto depended primarily on the attitude of the local bishop. The motu proprio *Summorum Pontificum* has fundamentally altered this dynamic, although (as we saw in the previous chapter) some bishops, or their liturgical advisors, do not seem to have grasped this.

The Society's aim was, and is to preserve and promote regular celebration of the Mass according to the older liturgical books, and in the Latin language. It is affiliated to Una Voce, an international organisation founded in 1966 (largely by members of the English LMS) to co-ordinate the activities of similar groups throughout the world (most take their name from this larger body: for example, Una Voce America, Una Voce Australia, Una Voce Scotland).

The LMS today remains very active in promoting and advertising celebrations of Mass according to the older books. It maintains a presence in every English and Welsh diocese, and publishes a quarterly magazine, *Mass of Ages*, which as well as news and articles of liturgical and traditionalist interest, also contains a comprehensive listing of the times and places throughout the country where the old Mass is celebrated with ecclesiastical approval, and contact details of the relevant local LMS representatives. Much of this information is also available via its website.

Despite its name, the Society's focus is on Mass in Latin according to the 1962 books, not Latin liturgy in general (the Association for Latin Liturgy, a distinct and rather smaller organisation, concentrates on encouraging celebrations of Mass in Latin according to the newer form of the Roman Rite[30]).

The LMS has also recently started to organise training days for clergy wishing to learn how to celebrate Mass according to the 1962 books. It is the obvious first point of contact for anyone in England and Wales interested in the older form of Mass.

Priestly Fraternity of St Peter (FSSP)

This is, under canon Law, a Clerical Society of Apostolic Life of Pontifical Right - that is, an association of priests not bound by vows, subject to the authority of diocesan bishops as regards their pastoral work, but formally answerable only to the Pope (via the Pontifical Commission Ecclesia Dei). It was founded in 1988 by a dozen ex-SSPX priests and twenty or so seminarians who declined to join Lefebvre in schism. They run two seminaries (in Bavaria and Nebraska) and have now almost two hundred priests

---

[30] See their website, *www.latin-liturgy.org*, for details.

and over a hundred seminarians; they operate worldwide, celebrating the liturgy according to the 1962 books. They have a small presence in Britain.

Centre International d'Etudes Liturgiques (CIEL)

Founded in 1994 by a group of French laypeople under the patronage of Cardinals Stickler and Oddi. They run an annual scholarly conference (referred to as a colloquium), the proceedings of which are usually published. CIEL should not be confused with its *bête noire*, ICEL (the International Commission for English in the Liturgy), who are responsible for the official (and hitherto often woefully deficient) translations of liturgical texts used in the English-speaking world.

Their British branch, CIEL UK, organises the translation and publication of the English version of their conference proceedings.

Sons of the Most Holy Redeemer
(formerly the Transalpine Redemptorists)

Originally founded in 1988 on the Isle of Sheppey by an Australian Redemptorist with links to the Ukrainian Rite, this is an order of men living a monastic life according to the spirit of St Alphonsus Liguori, and celebrating Mass according to the older Roman Rite and the Eastern Rite. They are now located at Papa Stronsay in the Orkneys, and are twenty or so strong (priests and professed brothers).

Despite their name, they have no formal link to the Redemptorist Order. From their foundation, they were closely associated with the SSPX. In June 2008, Pope Benedict accepted their request to be reconciled to the Holy See, and lifted all canonical sanctions against them. They recently opened another monastery in New Zealand. They have hitherto edited and published *The Catholic*, an SSPX house journal which combines solid traditional piety with occasional shrill polemic against the Conciliar reforms.

Organisations Worldwide

Personal Apostolic Administration of St John Mary Vianney

After the implementation of the post-Conciliar liturgical reforms, the then Bishop of Campos in Brazil, Antonio de Castro Mayer, declined to carry out the reforms within his diocese, where the older form of the Rite continued to be celebrated. Those clergy of the diocese who agreed with their Bishop on this matter formed themselves into the Priestly Union of St John Mary Vianney, an informal diocesan association. Throughout the 1970s and 80s, there was fairly close and regular contact between Castro Mayer and his clergy and Lefebvre's SSPX. In 1988, Castro Mayer joined Lefebvre in his illicit consecration of four bishops for the SSPX, an action which arguably incurred automatic excommunication, although the focus of Rome's disciplinary documents was on Lefebvre and the SSPX. The traditionalist priests of Campos chose one of their number, Licinio Rangel, to succeed Castro Mayer on his death in 1991; he was consecrated, without Papal mandate, in July of that year by three SSPX bishops - Tissier de Mallerais, Galaretta, and Williamson. This irregular situation continued until 2000 when, during the Jubilee Year, some of the Campos clergy visited Rome, and met Cardinal Castrillon Hoyos of the Ecclesia Dei Commission. The following August, the dissident clergy of the diocese wrote to Pope John Paul II acknowledging his primacy and requesting reconciliation. In December, John Paul II accepted their submission and lifted the censure on their Bishop, Rangel. In January of 2002 the Pope formally established the Personal Apostolic Administration of St John Mary Vianney, incorporating those clergy of Campos into a society under the authority of their own Bishop, authorised to celebrate the liturgy according to the older books. This Administration represents perhaps a third of the active clergy of the Diocese of Campos, the remainder of whom use the newer liturgical books. In late 2002, the Pope appointed Fernando Rifan as Bishop Rangel's co-adjutor; he succeeded as Bishop of the Administration when Rangel died in December 2002. Priests from the Administration are active in offering the older form of Mass in dioceses throughout Brazil. Bishop Rifan acts as an unofficial figurehead and spokesman for traditionalist Catholics worldwide.

Institute of Christ the King Sovereign Priest

Founded in 1990 to preserve and foster traditional Latin rite liturgy, art and music, by two French priests with the encouragement of Cardinal Silvio Oddi, and originally incardinated within Gabon in Africa, as part of the Francophone missionary church there. It now has thirty-five houses in ten countries (including five in the American Mid-West and one in California), fifty priests and roughly sixty seminarians, with their headquarters and seminary in Gricigliano in Tuscany. There is as yet no formal presence of the Institute in Britain.

Institute of the Good Shepherd

Founded in September 2006 by a number of priests expelled, or resigned, from the SSPX, this organisation made submission to the Holy See and agreed to accept the validity of the Second Vatican Council and the newer Rite of Mass, whilst retaining their own exclusive adherence to the older form. They have perhaps two dozen priest members, and a roughly similar number in seminary formation. They are mainly based in France, although there are small houses of the Institute in Chile, Brazil and Colombia.

Foundations in the United States

Apart from the recently reconciled Redemptorists, there are as yet no established Old Rite communities in Britain. In America, however, several small foundations have recently been set up; there are also branches of some of the organisations mentioned above.

Canons Regular of St John Cantius (SJC)

Founded in Chicago in 1998, they are based in the parish of St John Cantius in that city, live under the Augustinian Rule, and celebrate both the 1962 Rite and the newer liturgy. They are currently only twenty-four in number, but have the support of the Archbishop of Chicago, Cardinal George, and host an English-language website offering instruction in the older Rite (*www.sanctamissa.org*) and have a particular interest in Gregorian chant.

Canons Regular of the New Jerusalem

Another group living under the Augustinian rule who celebrate Mass in the older form. Based in Chesterfield, Missouri, they were founded in 2002 by Archbishop Raymond Burke of St Louis. Even smaller than the SJC, they have currently only three professed members.

Monks of the Most Blessed Virgin Mary of Mount Carmel

Historically, most Carmelites have lived as friars, with a mixed apostolate of contemplation and apostolic work. This community in Wyoming, however, has a purely contemplative charism, based around the older Liturgy and Office. They support themselves by roasting, blending and selling coffee beans. Founded in 2002, the community is currently seven strong.

There are also a number of houses of nuns in the United States who use the older form of the Liturgy, in Nebraska, Massachusetts and elsewhere.

French Monasteries using the Traditional Rite

The Abbey of St Madeleine de Le Barroux

This community of Benedictine monks was founded in the 1970s as a restoration of an abandoned monastery in the Vaucluse, near Avignon in the South of France. The monastery is dedicated to the celebration of the older liturgy. Because no French bishop was willing to ordain monks as priests to serve the community, their founder Dom Gérard Calvet approached Archbishop Lefebvre, who was happy to oblige. After the illicit 1988 consecrations, however, the monastic community of Le Barroux was unwilling to follow Lefebvre into formal schism, and was reconciled to the Church shortly thereafter. The community continues to flourish; it now has roughly seventy monks, a daughter house in Lot-et-Garonne, a sister house of nuns, and is a noted centre of liturgical scholarship. Abbot Calvet died in February 2008.

The Abbey of Notre-Dame de Fontgombault

In 1948 twenty-two monks from the Benedictine Abbey of Solesmes (notable for its devotion to the revival of

Gregorian chant) started a monastic house on the site of a disused Benedictine monastery on the banks of the river Creuse, in Berry in central France. They have retained the use of the older liturgy and chant. The community now numbers over a hundred monks, and has in its turn founded three daughter houses: the Abbeys of Randol (1971) and Triors (1984) and the Priory of Gaussan (1994), all in France; and Clear Creek Priory in the Ozark Mountains, Oklahoma (1999).

Fraternity of St Vincent Ferrer

Founded in 1979, this organisation celebrates Mass according to the Dominican Rite and has requested affiliation to the Dominican Order, although they have currently no formal connexion with them. They began as sedeprivationists (an obscure variant of sedevacantism devised by a French Dominican) but late in 1988 reconciled to Rome and were established as a Religious Institute of Pontifical Right. They have a small house in north-west France, from where they run retreats, summer camps and a small publishing house.

In addition, here are several other French monastic communities attached to the older Liturgy; but the above are the best-known. Alongside the monasteries of men, there are numerous French houses of nuns from traditionalist orders, who retain older forms of the religious habit and the liturgy. These include Benedictines at Jouques, Le Barroux and Rosans, and Dominican sisters at Baffe, Draguignan, Nantes, Pontcalec, and St Cloud.

The Chartres Pilgrimage

Another traditionalist event which attracts much interest is an annual pilgrimage from Paris to Chartres, which arrives after a week's cross-country walking in time for Solemn High Mass on the feast of Pentecost. Although it is, in origin, and predominant numbers, a French affair (it was founded by Abbot Calvet of Le Barroux), there is usually a sizeable English-speaking contingent from Britain and elsewhere.

Schismatics and Other Irregular Groups

It is in the nature of schism to reproduce itself by fission. This chapter considers mainly Archbishop Lefebvre's foundation, the Society of St Pius X[31]. Inevitably, however, elements within this schismatic group, or sympathetic to it, have judged it wanting in one particular or another of supposed orthodoxy. The resulting fractures have left dozens of smaller bodies splintered from the original outfit, often anathematising each other with remarkable vigour. Some of the better-known are mentioned below.

The Society of St Pius X (SSPX)

For many, the Society of St Pius X represents traditionalist Catholicism, in all its good and bad aspects. As we have seen in the previous chapter, there are very numerous alternatives for those attached to the older liturgical books; what is distinctive about the SSPX, and ultimately what led to its falling into schism from Rome, is a quite distinct, and at bottom unCatholic, attitude towards authority and tradition.

---

[31] Some, including some prominent clergy, have claimed that the SSPX is not, formally, in schism; however it is clear that its Bishops emphatically, and its clergy probably, are; the status of its lay adherents is debatable but certainly irregular. For ease of reference, they are here called schismatic without further qualification. I discuss this question more fully at the end of this section.

A Brief history

In 1968, some French seminarians in Rome with traditionalist sympathies, studying at the French-speaking college of Santa Chiara, met Marcel Lefebvre, a retired missionary Archbishop who had spent much of his life in Francophone Africa. They recognised in him a more traditional view of the priesthood and Catholicism than what they (perhaps not unfairly) saw as the lax, tending to unorthodox, formation on offer in many French (and other) seminaries of that period. In September 1969, nine seminarians approached Lefebvre and asked him to superintend their priestly formation. In October of the following year, Lefebvre received permission from the local Bishop to open a house of formation in Ecône, Switzerland. He also founded the Society of St Pius X, which was recognised by the local Bishop as a *pia unio* - under the then *Code of Canon Law*, an informal association without vows. Lefebvre probably desired a more permanent and official status for his organisation (probably that of a Society of Clerics without public vows, which would give it standing throughout the Church, not simply within one diocese), but it never received any formal recognition at any level higher than the diocesan.

During the early 1970s, comparatively large numbers of seminarians applied, and were accepted, to join the SSPX; and this at a time when mainstream diocesan seminaries in

France were emptying, and large numbers of priests and religious (there, as elsewhere) were laicised.

By 1974, some of the French hierarchy were unsettled by this, especially by Lefebvre's insistence not just on retaining, but on the exclusive use of the older liturgical books (the so-called Tridentine Rite, or 1962 Missal). This insistence, and Lefebvre's use of a distinctly old-fashioned model of what priestly ministry consisted in, and the theology underlying it, might, it was thought, lead to his establishing a pastoral organisation parallel to, and in conflict with, the existing Catholic Church in France. They were, in short, concerned that a schism might develop. On the other hand, it cannot be denied that the intellectual formation and moral climate in many diocesan seminaries, and religious novitiates, was at this period often woeful, and it is hardly surprising if those looking for a more traditional or robust formation were drawn to Lefebvre's organisation[32].

To try to settle these concerns, Pope Paul VI formed a commission of Cardinals to examine Lefebvre's movement and its seminary. They conducted an apostolic visitation in November 1974. Lefebvre took exception to an overheard remark by one of the visitors, whom he seems to have decided held heretical "modernist" views. On 21st

---

[32] For a good, if polemical account of the analogous situation in the United States at this time, and later, see Michael Rose's *Goodbye, Good Men* (Regnery, 2002).

November 1974 he published a Declaration questioning the authenticity of the Church's teaching, and denouncing the Vatican Council.

> "We refuse and have always refused," he wrote, "to follow the Rome of neo-Modernist and neo-Protestant tendencies such as were clearly manifested during the Second Vatican Council, and after the Council in all resulting reforms.
>
> All these reforms have indeed contributed and still contribute to the demolition of the Church, to the ruin of the priesthood, to the destruction of the Holy Sacrifice of the Mass and the sacraments, to the disappearance of the religious life, and to naturalistic and Teilhardian teaching in universities, seminaries, and catechesis, a teaching born of liberalism and Protestantism many times condemned by the solemn magisterium of the Church. No authority, even the very highest in the hierarchy, can constrain us to abandon or diminish our Catholic Faith such as it has been clearly expressed and professed by the Church's magisterium for nineteen centuries.[33]"

Clearly, attachment to the older forms of the Mass and to a more rigorous manner of priestly formation is one thing; wholesale rejection of an Ecumenical Council of the

---

[33] Quoted by Madrid & Vere, *More Catholic Than*, pp.35-36.

Church and defiance of the Pope is quite another. Lefebvre can hardly have expected this public fulmination to pass unnoticed, or without consequences; nor did it.

The local Bishop decided he must withdraw the approval his predecessor had granted to the SSPX; this was confirmed by the Congregation for Religious, and communicated to Lefebvre on 6th May 1975.

Lefebvre however claimed that the SSPX's status was in fact that of a Society of Clerics without public vows, which, under Canon Law, could not be suppressed except from Rome; this claim is frankly improbable on several grounds, as we have already seen. Even were this true, however, and the local Bishop had acted beyond his competence, on the very same day - 6th May - a Commission of cardinals, acting on the basis of the previous visitation and especially of Lefebvre's declaration of November 1974, also wrote to Lefebvre. They informed him that, with the declared support of the Pope, the local Bishop had been fully authorised to suppress the SSPX and its seminary. Even, therefore, were Lefebvre's claim of a more permanent status for the SSPX accurate, the local Bishop had been clearly delegated the authority to suppress it.

Not surprisingly, Lefebvre was unhappy with this turn of events and appealed to the Apostolic Signatura, the Church's highest court of appeal. It confirmed all that the Bishop, and the Commission, had done; Pope Paul himself added a personal letter to Lefebvre re-iterating this. There can be no doubt that, in the eyes of the Church, the SSPX and its seminary were definitively suppressed in May 1975.

Lefebvre, in effect, ignored all this. He continued the formation of his seminarians who, in the usual course of things, were due to proceed to priestly ordination in the summer of 1976. Lefebvre announced his intention of ordaining them, and incardinating them into the SSPX: this, under Canon Law, would mean that they were responsible to him as Bishop, not the local ordinary of wherever they were; although, since the SSPX was not, nor had it ever been, a recognised religious order or institution, this was a canonically impossible procedure. Here, again, Lefebvre was simply disobedient; the Vatican Secretary of State informed him, via the Papal Nuncio in Switzerland, that he should not proceed with the ordinations and, were he to do so, he would be automatically suspended from conferring orders. Lefebvre again protested, and was again told that it was the Pope's specific intention that he should not ordain his seminarians. To do so would incur suspension from conferring orders for him, and from saying Mass or celebrating any other sacraments for anyone he should ordain. Despite all this, Lefebvre went ahead and ordained his first SSPX priests on 29th June 1976.

The next day, as anticipated, the Holy See announced that Lefebvre had been suspended from conferring Holy Orders for a year; and that those he had ordained priests were suspended from exercising their priesthood. Despite what Lefebvre said at the time, and he and his apologists have said subsequently, these disciplinary measures were not taken because he had ordained priests to say Mass in the older form; but in response to an act of deliberate and conscious disobedience to the Church's authority.

Two weeks later, Lefebvre received a formal warning from the Congregation for Bishops that he should take immediate action to repair the scandal he had caused, or be subject to further canonical penalties. In reply, Lefebvre wrote to Pope Paul VI. Some sentences from his letter give an idea of its tone:

> "Let Your Holiness abandon that ill-omened undertaking of compromise with the ideas of modern man, an undertaking which originates in a secret understanding between high dignitaries in the Church and those of Masonic lodges since before the Council... To persevere in that direction is to pursue the destruction of the Church. Your Holiness will easily understand that we cannot collaborate in so calamitous a purpose, which we should do were we to close our seminaries."[34]

Needless to say, this letter was not the response needed; rather, it merely added to obstinate formal disobedience a shrill, and frankly bizarre, allegation against the Pope himself. On 22nd July, the Congregation for Bishops suspended Lefebvre *a divinis* - that is, from exercising any

---

[34]   Quoted in Madrid & Vere, *More Catholic Than*, p.54.

and all priestly faculties whatever - absolution from which suspension is reserved to the Holy Father personally.

Over the next twelve years, there were desultory negotiations with various Roman dicasteries about regularising the SSPX's situation. Meanwhile Lefebvre continued to ordain men as priests: ordinations that were valid, but not licit. After some years of desultory negotiation, principally with Cardinal Ratzinger of the CDF (now Pope Benedict XVI), Lefebvre and the Cardinal signed a protocol agreement on 5th May 1988. This essentially regularised the SSPX's position: it was to be established as a clerical society of apostolic life of Pontifical right. This, in effect, would make the SSPX something analogous to a religious order, responsible to the Pope alone, and outside the normal jurisdiction of local bishops.

The Holy See agreed to lift all suspensions from SSPX clergy, to allow the use of the 1962 Missal, and permit Lefebvre to consecrate one SSPX bishop to allow ordinations and confirmations in the traditional Rite. In return, the SSPX was to accept Vatican II, and the reformed Liturgy, as authentically Catholic; and agree to supervision by a Roman Commission of five members, two of them from the SSPX itself (including their putative bishop).

Within three weeks, however, Lefebvre had a change of heart. He wrote to the Cardinal expressing concern that the SSPX would be incorporated into the "Conciliar Church" if the Commission did not contain a majority from "Tradition" (that is, the SSPX) and furthermore that no fewer than three SSPX bishops were consecrated. He signalled his intention to consecrate bishops unilaterally if his demands were not met. Ratzinger's reply pointed out that, in the first place, the Commission would always act under obedience to the Pope and could not in any sense be seen as a determinative body of itself; and, second, that consecrating bishops without Papal mandate would be a very grave act, formally constitutive of schism. Lefebvre refused to back down. Despite Rome's willingness to re-open negotiations even at the eleventh hour, on 30th June 1988, Lefebvre performed the illicit consecrations of four SSPX priests as Bishops, assisted by Bishop Antonio de Castro Mayer, retired Bishop of Campos, Brazil. On 2nd July, Pope John Paul II declared Lefebvre and his four bishops (Bernard Fellay, Richard Williamson, Bernard Tissier de Mallerais, and Alfonso Galaretta) schismatic, and thus excommunicated.

Lefebvre died in March 1991, Castro Mayer a month later; neither was formally reconciled[35]. There have been subsequent desultory negotiations between Rome and the rump SSPX, but none as yet have borne fruit, largely because of the SSPX's obduracy in refusing to admit either the Vatican Council or the validity of liturgical reform. The SSPX's current superior, Bernard Fellay, was thought

---

[35] For the subsequent history of Castro Mayer's followers, and their reconciliation with Rome, see p.35 above.

54

more inclined to compromise than some of his colleagues, particularly Richard Williamson, although in a public letter dated 19th April 2008 Fellay declined reconciliation with Rome despite *Summorum Pontificum*, on the grounds that the Church refused to disavow the documents of the Vatican Council. It is, in any event, likely than any reconciliation would provoke a further schism within the SSPX itself. In late June 2008 reports reached the press that, in the context of a request from the SSPX for the lifting of canonical sanctions against them, the PCED had named a number of conditions that the SSPX must accept before any future dialogue could be meaningful[36]. These conditions themselves are contextual to any substantive agreement; this, as in 1988, would have to include accepting the validity of the reformed Rite of Mass and of the Second Vatican Council, and would likely entail the SSPX's erection as a form of personal prelature (analogous to the position enjoyed by Opus Dei). Public responses from various SSPX *prominenti* seemed to indicate a reluctance to accept these conditions. At time of writing, it is unclear what if anything will come from this development.

There are, today, something between four hundred and fifty and five hundred active SSPX priests; the precise

---

[36] They included committing to a response proportionate to the Pope's generosity, to avoiding public criticism of him, ceasing to claim access to a Magisterium superior to the Pope's, being willing to act charitably and with respect for the Pope's authority; and finally to reply to these conditions before the end of June 2008.

number of lay adherents is unclear. The highest estimates claim a million followers; others as low as 200,000. There is little reliable evidence in the public domain that could be evaluated or quantified, but the truth is probably somewhere towards the lower end of this scale.

A Note about Excommunication and Schism

A state of schism is not something trivial, or purely formal; the Church Fathers describe it as "a wound in the Body of Christ". But what, exactly, is the status of the SSPX? The motu proprio *Ecclesia Dei* of 1988 explicitly stated that Lefebvre and those he consecrated bishops were in schism and thus excommunicated[37].This also extended to any clergy and laity who "adhere to the schism". There has never been any formal statement of what this adherence might consist in, but some rules of thumb can be applied,

---

[37] Par. 3 of the motu proprio describes the ordinations as "a schismatic act" and refers to Canon 751 of the *Code of Canon Law*, which defines schism as "the withdrawal of submission to the Supreme Pontiff or from communion with the members of the Church subject to him". The letter later (par. 5c) declares "Everyone should be aware that formal adherence to the schism is a grave offence against God and carries the penalty of excommunication decreed by the Church's law". A Decree from the Congregation of Bishops annexed to the motu proprio re-iterated this, saying, "The priests and faithful are warned not to support the schism of Monsignor Lefebvre, otherwise they shall incur *ipso facto* the very grave penalty of excommunication". The precise definition of what "adherence" or "support" was not then given; on the basis of subsequent advice from the Ecclesia Dei Commission, however, it seems to be as outlined in the body of the text above.

in the light of public statements later made by the Ecclesia Dei Commission. The status of SSPX clergy is fairly clear: membership of a society whose head (for the past twenty years) has been an excommunicated bishop, and whose public stance includes a wholesale condemnation of the Church since the Second Vatican Council, almost certainly constitutes adherence to schism. The status of the laity is more complicated; simply attending an SSPX Mass, which may be done for a number of reasons, is probably not of itself enough to qualify as adherence; but the more often one does this, the more likely it is that one will adopt the schismatic mentality that refuses submission to the Pope and communion with those who accept his authority. Those who do so may be supposed to adhere to schism in this formal sense. Whilst one need not suppose, then, that occasional attendance at an SSPX Mass has put one into a state of schism, exclusive or habitual attendance runs a high risk of this grave consequence.

SSPX literature often makes several claims in this connexion:

1) that attending their Masses fulfils the Sunday obligation. Strictly speaking, this is true: it is Mass celebrated in a Catholic Rite. However attending a schismatic Mass can only be considered advisable if there is no easily accessible non-schismatic alternative, either in the older or newer form of the Rite; nor, if one does attend

a schismatic Mass (for a baptism or similar occasion, for instance) should one receive Communion.

Note, moreover, that a priest requires proper authority from a bishop validly to hear confessions and conduct marriages; SSPX priests do not have these faculties, so these sacraments celebrated by them are not valid. A confession heard *in extremis* by an SSPX priest, or made by someone ignorant of his canonical status, would however be valid, since in such circumstances *ecclesia supplet* - even a laicised priest can give valid absolution under these conditions.

2) that Cardinal Castrillon Hoyos of the PCED affirmed in March 2004 that they were not schismatic. There is no public record of this statement or the context in which it was made; the judgement that the SSPX's Bishops and clergy (at least) are schismatic was made by the Holy See, and absolution from it is reserved to the Holy See alone. Until the Pope says the schism is ended, we may assume it persists. Any private statements on this issue by Cardinal Castrillon Hoyos to the contrary are simply that: private opinions. As has been made clear above, the original documents of 1988 are explicit in naming Lefebvre's "schism"; quite how this schism persists in regard to individual clergy and laity can only be judged on an individual basis. But the original decree also named the four illicitly consecrated Bishops; they at very least must

be assumed to be in schism, and their adherents similarly in proportion to their attachment to the SSPX.

The Historical Background of French Traditionalism

Observers in the English-speaking world may find it difficult to understand the depth of hostility to the traditional Mass found amongst many of the French hierarchy and clergy, and to account for Lefebvre's and the SSPX's odd obsession with Freemasons, with conspiratorial views of history, and its general vehemence. Without giving a comprehensive account of French history since the Revolution, it is important to know that the SSPX in France draws much support from right-wing and legitimist (that is, monarchist) circles. Historically, those holding these views were much involved with the wartime Vichy regime of Marshal Pétain, and before that with Action Française, a hard-right notionally Catholic movement (founded by the atheist Charles Maurras) that mixed integrist (that is, doctrinally hyper-correct) theology with anti-Semitism and suspicion of Freemasonry (both legacies of the political climate of France at the start of the twentieth century).

There are numerous links between the French political right and the SSPX, links both personal and ideological. In 1985, Archbishop Lefebvre endorsed the Front National leader Jean-Marie Le Pen as a candidate for the French Presidency; as, in 1991, did the then SSPX priest Fr Philippe Laguerie (he is now Superior of the Institute of the Good Shepherd). Lefebvre himself was legitimist in his political opinions, broadly supportive of absolute monarchy, and spoke approvingly of the "Catholic order" of the Vichy regime. In July 1991, a Solemn Requiem Mass was celebrated at St Nicholas-du-Chardonnet (a Parisian church occupied by the SSPX, in defiance of the French hierarchy, since 1977) for the repose of the soul of Philippe Pétain on the fortieth anniversary of his death[38]. Two years earlier, Paul Touvier, a former member of the Vichy paramilitary Milice, wanted for ordering the killing of seven Jewish hostages in 1944, was run to earth at an SSPX house in Nice. He was eventually sentenced to life imprisonment for crimes against humanity.

The SSPX has always been a primarily French phenomenon, although it does have a widely cast presence elsewhere. It has, to some extent, clearly become a haven for many nostalgic for the political attitudes of Action Française, and a type of militant "state Catholicism" often advocated by them or by similar groups. The persistent fulminations by the SSPX hierarchy against the Protestant-Jewish-Freemasonical "heresies" of the Second Vatican Council complete the picture. For people of this mentality,

---

[38] There may well have been earlier, and subsequent, similar Requiems. There is certainly an annual Requiem for Pétain celebrated at the church of St Eloi in Bordeaux, formerly an SSPX outpost but now run by the Institute of the Good Shepherd. I do not want to imply that Mass should not be offered for Pétain, or similar figures; merely that the prominence given it is suggestive.

the primary issue is no longer the Liturgy, but an entire ecclesiological approach, in which they set themselves at odds with the mainstream of Catholic theology both now and throughout history. This is not to say that this means French bishops are justified in seeing behind any request for Mass to be celebrated according to the older books the full panoply of Maurrasite or Pétainist ideology, or to suppose that all devotees of the older Rite come from this particular, and peculiar, political viewpoint; but one can perhaps understand how, in the light of the recent history of the Church in France, the confusion could easily be made.

The SSPX and Judaism

The texts of the Second Vatican Council take great care to acknowledge and express the Church's attitude of respect towards the Jewish religion and people, and to stress the enduring, and to Christianity central, value of their Scriptures and witness. The key text is the decree *Nostra Aetate*, which sets out the Church's attitude to non-Christian religions. An important part of this document deals with Judaism. It clearly affirms the abiding nature of Israel's election by God: "the apostle Paul maintains that the Jews remain very dear to God, for the sake of the patriarchs, since God does not take back the gifts he bestowed or the choice he made." (par.4; see *Romans*, 11:28-29) *Nostra Aetate*, too, is at pains to disown two pernicious distortions of the Christian attitude towards Judaism that were once frequently espoused by some Christian, or nominally Christian writers. The critical paragraph is this:

> "Even though the Jewish authorities and those who followed their lead pressed for the death of Christ (cf *John* 19:6), neither all Jews indiscriminately at that time, nor Jews today, can be charged with the crimes committed during his passion. It is true that the Church is the new people of God, yet the Jews should not be spoken of as rejected or accursed as if this followed from holy Scripture."

This is an explicit rejection, by the Church's solemn Magisterium as represented by an Ecumenical Council, both of the charge of Deicide sometimes made against the Jewish people, and of so-called Replacement Theology, which holds that God's Covenant with Moses and the Jewish people was utterly void and nullified by their failure corporately to recognise Jesus as the promised Messiah. These views have, in fact, neither of them ever been held by the authentic teaching body of the Church as true; but there have not been wanting theologians and others at many different historical periods who have asserted that one or the other of these claims, or even both of them, were necessary corollaries to the Gospel. The cover that these fundamentally un-Christian claims has given to anti-Semitic prejudice or violence is a matter of grievous historical record. No Catholic Christian, however, has now any excuse for claiming any sanction on the part of the Church for these noxious libels.

Several of the leaders of the SSPX, however, make this very text from *Nostra Aetate* a reason to reject the Council. This is not to say that all, or many of the SSPX's clergy or lay adherents are conscious anti-Semites, if they ever even consider this issue; but elements of their leadership have publicly made statements that, at very least, are careless of what the Church has solemnly affirmed in this matter. I do not wish to dwell on this point, but will simply quote from a widely circulated pamphlet containing the text of a conference given by Fr Franz Schmidberger, sometime Superior General of the SSPX:

> "It is also clear that the Jews of our day cannot be called our elder brothers in the faith. How could the Pope say such a thing when he visited the synagogue in Rome three years ago?

> There is one other question. Can we say that the Jews are guilty of Deicide? We must say yes because it is they who asked for our Lord's death and called for His blood upon their heads and the heads of their children. I want to make it very clear: I do not speak about the Jews as a race, I speak about the Jews as a religion. So what about the Jews of our day? Well, as long as they do not withdraw from this crime, from this action of their ancestors, they are also guilty of it. They must

disassociate themselves from it and recognise our Lord; they must be baptised and become his disciples."[39]

Similar statements have been made by another prominent SSPXer, Bishop Richard Williamson (one of the four consecrated by Lefebvre in 1988). Williamson has for a while had some notoriety on the internet, and more recently in the English Catholic press, as an unconsciously comic turn. An Englishman (a Wykehamist and Cambridge man) Williamson stands at an identifiable extreme of the SSPX's leadership. He denies that the Holocaust happened, believes in the authenticity of the notorious forgery *The Protocols of the Elders of Zion*[40], claims the September 11th atrocities were the work of the American government, that society (and the Church) is in the grip of Freemasons and international Jewish finance, that women wearing trousers is the primary cause of homosexuality in men, and that the musical *The Sound of Music* is "latent pornography". One's first conclusion might be that the SSPX is a powerful magnet

---

[39] *Time Bombs of the Second Vatican Council* by Franz Schmidberger, Angelus Press 1996, 2005, p.20-21. The entire text is a systematic attack on the major Conciliar documents.

[40] An anti-Semitic tract purporting to present the secret Jewish plan for world domination, it has been a favourite resort of Jew-baiters both amateur and professional since it first appeared in 1903. It was very probably confected by the Tsar's secret police. Its long-suspected status as a forgery was conclusively established in 1938 by Pierre Charles SJ, an associate of Henri de Lubac.

for the barking mad; but given the French context we have reviewed above, some at least of his views may appear in a different light.

The Church has consistently taught that God's revelation to the Jewish people has enduring value. To suppose, as many Catholics once did, and as some in the SSPX still seem to do, that Christianity can be as it were detached from its roots in Judaism, is simple madness. As Henri de Lubac forcibly insisted in a series of articles written during the Second World War, at the height of the Vichy collaboration and in response to fantastic schemes to discover a supposed "Aryan Christianity" rid from all taint of Jewishness, anti-Semitism of this type, and indeed of any type, is in fact anti-Christianity. As the Church asserted in the second and third centuries in the face of the claims by the heretical bishop Marcion and his followers that the Old Testament should be removed from the Canon, without the enduring heritage of the Hebrew Scriptures, and the religious context of Judaism, the New Testament and Christian belief cannot exist.

Sedevacantists and Conclavists

A common refuge of the ecclesiologically disaffected throughout history has been to assume that a specific Pope with whom they have a doctrinal or disciplinary difference is, by virtue of his opposition to them, the privileged possessors of the truth, in fact no Pope at all.

The logical corollary to this claim is to hold that the See of Peter is for the moment vacant; hence the general name for this type of believer is sedevacantist. Although the SSPX as a whole recognises the papacy as genuine if (by their lights) mistaken, there are doubtless numerous individuals within "mainstream" schismatic groups such as the SSPX, or sympathetic to them, who hold these views privately. The late Fr Oswald Baker (ob. 2004), for example, the traditionalist priest of Downham Market in Norfolk who had some notoriety in the 1970s for his frequent clashes with the hierarchy, apparently ended as a sedevacantist. Currently active organisations with this bent include the Society of St Pius V (breakaway SSPXers), the Congregation of Mary Immaculate Queen (CMRI), and the Most Holy Family Monastery in New York State. They typically inhabit intemperate corners of the internet, and issue sporadic broadsides on the errors of Pope Benedict, Lefebvre, the SSPX and pretty much everyone except themselves. Bile of this quality can exercise a certain morbid fascination, but I would not advise looking it out.

A subset of this tendency are the Conclavists: those who, in addition to holding that the current Pope is no Pope, believe themselves authorised to fill the supposed vacancy with a candidate of their own choosing. Here we are on the wilder shores of ecclesiological lunacy. Various resultant antipopes exist, usually with negligible followings and politically and theologically eccentric opinions[41]. These are worth mentioning simply to alert those who are attracted to the older Rite to the need for caution in finding a Mass to attend.

Envoi

"Here, I would say, is what happens inevitably, if once the principle of Catholic unity is lost! All this confusion, this priggishness, this pedantry, this eccentricity and worse, follows directly from the rash step that takes you outside the fold of Peter!"

(Ronald Knox, *Enthusiasm*, p.v; explaining his original plan for the book)

---

[41] We may instance Manuel Corral, self-styled "Peter II", successor to Clemente Dominguez Gomez ("Gregory XVII"). Dominguez founded a pseudo-Carmelite order in 1975 (inspired by alleged apparitions of the Virgin Mary in El Palmar, a village in Andalucia), was illicitly ordained bishop by a Vietnamese archbishop (who was excommunicated for his pains) and then blinded in a car crash in 1976. On the death of Paul VI in 1978, Dominguez claimed Christ appeared to him and told him he was now Pope. He issued decrees canonizing Christopher Columbus and General Franco, publicly admitted persistent sexual misconduct in 1997, and died in 2005. His followers (not very numerous – perhaps two thousand worldwide) claimed he exhibited stigmata and frequently saw visions. Since 1983 the Palmarian sect has departed significantly from anything resembling Catholic liturgy and theology.

Conclusion - the Past and the Future

Since Pope Benedict issued his motu proprio *Summorum Pontificum*, there has been much speculation on the aim and scope of this reform. Is his attempt to make the older Rite of Mass more available simply a piece of nostalgia, a sop to those attached to a form of liturgy of mainly antiquarian interest, or a harking-back to the liturgical praxis of his youth?

Certainly there remain concerns amongst those attached to the older Rite that it and it alone is a standard of tradition and theological certainty. But, as I attempted to explain in my first chapter, there is nothing explicit or implicit in the reformed Rite that does not express precisely the same Mystery as the older form. Abrupt changes of liturgical style can, and did, cause acute pain to the faithful, and this is deeply to be regretted; as, also, are the abuses that persist in many celebrations of the newer Rite despite the Church's repeated efforts to quell them. But these things do not go to the heart of the Eucharist.

Fundamentally, this is a matter of obedience. The Holy See has repeatedly and solemnly affirmed the validity of the liturgical reforms that led to the revised Missal; nothing that Benedict has said to affirm the continuing value of the older form of Mass subverts or denies this. Those who continue to claim the older form of the Rite as the only valid form of Mass are, in their way, as guilty of dissent from the Magisterium as those self-proclaimed "liberal Catholics" who, after forty years, still ritually fulminate against the teaching of *Humanae Vitae*. In each case, an individual or group has identified a privileged area of (it may be) sincere, conscientious refusal to accept the Church's solemn teaching. No matter how sincere or heartfelt, dissent remains dissent, and is fundamentally unCatholic.

If, then, the reformed Rite is wholly valid and wholly Catholic, what is the point of celebrating the older form? Several answers may be given. One is that the Church has always valued legitimate diversity in its Rites; another, that the particular liturgical tradition that was summarised and codified at Trent has a historical, theological, and musical richness that should be valued and allowed to flourish; third, and perhaps most important, we should remember what Benedict has repeated said: there is only one Roman Rite. The crisis in the Church in recent decades is not, I have argued above, primarily a liturgical but a catechetical one; but insofar as it has a liturgical reflex, it has expressed itself in a loss of the sense of Tradition. The notion that the "new Mass" is a wholly new confection unmoored in any prior praxis of which we have firm historical record, and thus of its nature open to endless *ad libitum* variation on the part of "the People of God" is one that stubbornly persists amongst both its critics and its adherents. The Pope's intention in making the older form of the Mass universally available is, surely, to reinforce our understanding of the newer form as one anchored in the same Tradition as the old, to permit the mutual enrichment of both forms, and to allow us to recover our sense of the Liturgy as something wholly rooted in Tradition, something greater than ourselves and our whims or preferences, God's gift of Himself to us in Christ.

A Note on the Good Friday Prayers

For Easter 2008, Pope Benedict XVI released a text of a new prayer for the Jewish people to be used in the General Intercessions that form part of the Liturgy of Good Friday, replacing that formerly found in the 1962 liturgical books. There has been a certain amount of controversy arising from this, so it might be useful to present the facts of the case.

First, we need to remember what the General Intercessions are. It is a fundamental part, perhaps one might even say *the* fundamental part, of the Church's mission, drawn from that entrusted to the People of Israel, to make intercession for the world. The priestly people of God are called to pray on behalf of the world, to stand before God and present to him the whole world's needs, sorrows, and joys, as much as their own, to offer him praise, and to ask him to show his loving mercy to us all.

This is, of course, part of the daily mission - the job, if you like - of the Christian; as well as private prayer, the great public liturgies of the Church - principally the Eucharist, and the Divine Office or Liturgy of the Hours - make this constant intercession. On Good Friday, however, as part of the Triduum of Easter, the great Passover of the Lord, the highest liturgy of the Christian year, this role is made even more explicit in the solemn prayers of the General Intercessions. Here, the Church brings before God all the world's peoples and their concerns, both in general, and also particular groups for whom she has an especial care. Thus, non-Catholic Christians, atheists, political leaders, and the sick are also specifically prayed for, much as are the Jewish people.

The older prayer for the Jews had long been the single most-often cited piece of evidence for the supposed "anti-Semitism" of the older liturgy, and thus an indication of the entire form's unfitness in our climate of inter-religious dialogue. It is worth taking a brief look at the various texts before evaluating the justice of this charge.

The older prayers, found in the earliest printed editions (1570), originally read as follows:

Oremus et pro perfidis Iudaeis: ut Deus et Dominus noster auferat velamen de cordibus eorum; ut et ipsi agnoscant Iesum Christum Dominum nostrum

Omnipotens sempiterne Deus, qui etiam judaicam perfidiam a tua misericordia non repellis: exaudi preces nostras, quas pro illius populi obcaecatione deferimus; ut, agnita veritatis tuae luce, quae Christus est, a suis tenebris eruantur. Per eundem Dominum. Amen.

Literally translated, this means:

Let us pray also for the unbelieving Jews: that our God and Lord will remove the veil from their hearts, so that they too may acknowledge our Lord Jesus Christ.

Almighty, eternal God, who do not withold your mercy even from Jewish unbelief, heed the prayers that we offer for the blindness of that people, that they may acknowledge the light of your truth, which is Christ, and be delivered from their darkness: through the same. Amen.

The phrase here rendered "unbelieving Jews" is often wrongly translated "perfidious Jews"; whilst *perfidus* can mean "treacherous" in classical Latin, the context here (a prayer for faith) makes it clear that the equally attested, and weaker, sense "unbelieving" is the one intended here.

In 1959, Pope John XXIII, wanting to avoid even the possibility of giving offence, removed *perfidus* from the prayers. In the 1962 Mass books, then (the only form of the older Mass currently authorised to be said) the prayers read:

Oremus et pro Iudaeis: ut Deus [&c as before]

Omnipotens sempiterne Deus, qui Iudaeos etiam a tua misericordia [&c as before]

Let us pray also for the Jews: that our God [&c]

Almighty, eternal God, who do not withold your mercy even from the Jews, heed [&c]

The objection to the phrase "perfidious Jews", then, is doubly a canard: first, it depends on a contentious and arguably inaccurate translation of the Latin; secondly, it bases itself on an obsolete form of the text, no longer used anywhere (or, if it is used, done in defiance of express Papal instruction)[42].

Still, mindful of these disputes, Pope Benedict issued a revised text in February 2008, which must now be used instead of the prayer originally found in the 1962 Missal whenever the Liturgy of the Triduum is celebrated with the older books.

This new prayer is as follows:

Oremus et pro Iudaeis: ut Deus et Dominus noster illuminet corda eorum, ut agnoscant Iesum Christum salvatorem omnium hominum.

Omnipotens sempiterne Deus, qui vis ut omnes homines salvi fiant et ad agnitionem veritatis veniant, concede propitius, ut plenitudine gentium in Ecclesiam Tuam intrante omnis Israel salvus fiat. Per Christum Dominum nostrum. Amen.

---

[42] As a comparison, this is the text from the Roman Missal of 1970, in the current English translation: *Let us pray for the Jewish people, the first to hear the word of God, that they may continue to grow in the love of his name, and in faithfulness to his covenant. Almighty and eternal God, long ago you gave your promise to Abraham and his posterity. Listen to your Church as we pray that the people you first made your own may arrive at the fullness of redemption. Amen.* Even here, the prayer asks implicitly that the Jewish people may come to faith in Christ.

In English:

Let us pray for the Jews: that our Lord and God may enlighten their hearts so that they may recognise Jesus Christ as the saviour of all men.

Almighty, eternal God, who wish all men to be saved and to come to the recognition of truth, mercifully grant that, as the fullness of the nations enter into your Church, all Israel may be saved. Through Christ our Lord. Amen.

Rather subtly, although the revised text no longer refers explicitly to the "veil" over the hearts of the Jews, its use of the phrase "the fullness of the nations" is an allusion to Romans 11 vv25-26, which is a passage that refers explicitly to the "blindness of Israel" in front of the claims of Christ. However whilst it might be possible for an obstinate objector to find this allusion offensive, someone so minded would have to object to the whole thrust of St Paul's theology of Christ's covenant, and its relation to the covenant made with Moses. Moreover, the deep respect and reverence that a Christian owes Judaism, and the enduring witness of Jews to their faith in God's promise to them, does not, and should not mean that he must decline to affirm that the revelation of God in Christ is a fulfillment, and in a certain sense a passing beyond, of God's revelation in Judaism. We should affirm the truth of

Judaism, certainly; but also the greater truth of the person of Christ, which does not replace the former but does bring it to perfection. If we will not do the first, we deny an essential part of our faith, and also God's faithfulness to his people Israel; if we will not do the second, in what sense are we Christians at all? As the great text of the Vatican Council on relations with non-Christian religions, *Nostra Aetate*, puts it: "Yet she [the Church] proclaims and is in duty bound to proclaim without fail, Christ who is the way, the truth and the life". (par.2)

Further Information

Useful Organisations

The Latin Mass Society
11 - 13 Macklin Street, London, WC2B 5NH
Tel: 0207 404 7284 Fax: 0207 831 5585
E-mail: *thelatinmasssociety@snmail.co.uk*
Website: *www.latin-mass-society.org*

Priestly Fraternity of St Peter (FSSP) in Great Britain
8a Walgrave Road, London, SW5 0RL
Tel: 020 7159 0552 Website: *www.fssp.org.uk*

CIEL UK
83 Runshaw Lane, Euxton, Chorley, Lancashire, PR7 6AX
Email: *information@cieluk.org* Website: *www.cieluk.org*

Further Reading

Probably the first thing anyone interested in the older Rite of Mass will need is a Missal, or at least the Order of Mass. An excellent recent edition of the 1962 Missal is published by Baronius Press.

Details of many books useful for particular topics are given in footnotes to the relevant sections of the text. A complete bibliography of this subject would be enormous and probably unnavigable except by the already initiated. Some titles of general interest include:

Sacrosanctum Concilium with an introduction by Francis Cardinal Arinze (CTS, 2004)

More Catholic Than the Pope - An Inside Look at Extreme Traditionalism by Patrick Madrid and Pete Vere (OSV, 2004)

The Pope, the Council, and the Mass by James Likoudis and Kenneth D Whitehead (Emmaus Road, revised edition 2006)

The History of the Mass Explained by Charles Dilke (CTS, 2008)

The classic rubrical guide is Adrian Fortescue's *The Ceremonies of the Roman Rite Described* (revised J B O'Connell; St Michael's Abbey Press 2003)

A comparable book for the 1970 Rite would be Peter Elliott, *Ceremonies of the Modern Roman Rite* (revised edition, Ignatius Press, 2005)

Alcuin Reid's *The Organic Development of the Roman Liturgy* (Ignatius Press, 2005) is an important study of the background of liturgical reform

All these titles, and also the *Ordo* (liturgical calendar) for the 1962 Missal (which has a different schedule of feast-days from the newer Lectionary) are available from the CTS Bookshop near Westminster Cathedral:

CTS Bookshop, 25 Ashley Place, London, SW1P 1LT
Tel: 0207 834 1363 Email *bookshop@cts-online.org.uk*

Websites

There is a vast quantity of information relative to the older form of the Roman Rite, and bodies that promote it, available on the internet. As always with the interweb, one must exercise careful discrimination; much of this information is mischievous, inaccurate, partial, or plain wrong. Here, however, are some useful (and generally reliable) starting points.

New Liturgical Movement
A clearing-house blog for matters of liturgical interest, with strong traditionalist sympathies.
www.thenewliturgicalmovement.blogspot.com

What Does the Prayer Really Say? (WDTPRS)
Run by Fr John Zuhlsdorf, formerly of the Pontifical Commission Ecclesia Dei, this blog offers a well-informed commentary on liturgical issues from a traditionalist but mostly balanced standpoint. It is also an excellent source of general information on these matters. *www.wdtprs.com*

The Hermeneutic of Continuity
Fr Tim Finigan, parish priest of Blackfen in Kent (diocese of Southwark) is a well-known English blogger whose site is another good source of information on the older form of the Rite. *www.the-hermeneutic-of-continuity.blogspot.com*

The Carmelite monks of Wyoming have a site at *www.carmelitemonks.org*; you can buy their coffee at *www.mysticmonkcoffee.com*

The History of the Mass Explained

The Mass is the source and summit of Christian life and has been from the very beginning. As such, the way in which the Mass is celebrated is always under scrutiny. Arguments continue to rage about the relationship of the form of the Mass celebrated today to what has gone before. This booklet looks at how the Mass has changed and developed over time, and how at different times central control has been needed to remedy abuses while at other times local developments were fostered and allowed.

Fr Charles Dilke studied Architecture at Cambridge, became Catholic in 1960 and joined the Oratory in 1961. He has been a priest for over 40 years and is a Fellow of the Royal Astronomical Society.

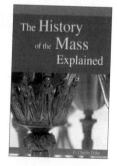

CTS Code: H 508

ISBN: 978 1 86082 482 1